Why Do We Say The Things We Say?

101 Fully Illustrated Explanations of the Things We All Say Every Day

Graham Hodson

Why Do We Say The Things We Say?

© Graham Hodson All Rights Reserved 2023

The moral right of the author has been asserted
First published by Rockwood Publishing 2023

All rights reserved. This book contains material protected under International and Federal Copyright Laws and Treaties.
Any unauthorized reprint or use of this material is strictly prohibited.

This book or parts thereof may not be reproduced in any form, stored in any information storage/retrieval system, or transmitted in any form by any means – electronic, mechanical, photocopy, recording, or otherwise – without prior and express written permission from the author and/or publisher.

Copyrighted © 2023

Contents

Introduction 1

Rule Of Thumb 2

As Mad As A Hatter 4

Bluetooth 6

On Cloud 9 8

Money For Old Rope 12

Upper Hand 6

A Quick Buck 14

Peeping Tom 16

Let Your Hair Down 18

Kick The Bucket 20

Get The Sack 22

The Whole 9 Yards 24

Don't Look a Gift-Horse in the Mouth 26

Pardon My French 28

Filthy Rich 30

Go Bananas 32

Happy as Larry 34

Kangaroo Court 36

My Ears Are Burning 38

Nineteen to the Dozen 40

On the Fiddle 42

Sick as a Parrot 44

Takes the Biscuit/Takes the Cake 46

A Vicious Circle 48

Walls Have Ears 50

All Bells and Whistles 52

You Can Lead a Horse to Water, But You Can't Make It Drink 54

In the Doghouse 56

I'll Eat My Hat 58

A Bun In the Oven 60

A Fish Out of Water 62

Right-Hand Man 64

A Bird in the Hand is Worth Two in the Bush 66

Knock the Spots Off 68

Sheriff 70

Eavesdropping 72

Butter Someone Up 74

Let The Cat Out Of The Bag 76

Pull Your Socks Up 78

Spill The Beans 80

A Flash In The Pan 82

Dead Ringer 84

Last-Ditch Attempt 86

Paint The Town Red 88

Hell For Leather 90

Caught Red-Handed... 92

Out Of The Blue 94

Stinking Rich 96

At The Drop Of A Hat... 98

A Feather In Your Cap.. 100

Quantum Leap... 102

A Red Letter Day 104

On A Wing And A Prayer 106

The $64,000 Question 108

In Seventh Heaven 110

Close, But No Cigar 112

Catch 22 114

Carry The Can... 116

Okay/OK.. 118

As Bright As A Button 120

Off The Cuff 122

Laughing Stock.. 124

Once In A Blue Moon 126

Son Of A Gun 128

Break A Leg... 130

Spin Doctor... 132

Spitting Image 134

The Living Daylights 136

A Barrel Of Laughs	138
Beat A Hasty Retreat	140
Zig Zag	142
In The Doldrums	144
Pay Through The Nose	146
Long-Winded	148
The Real McCoy	150
Dressed Up To The Nines	152
Gift Of The Gab	154
Hedge Your Bets	156
Give Up The Ghost	158
Wooden Spoon	160
Red Herring	162
Pound Of Flesh	164
Bite The Bullet	166
Draw A Blank	168
Dutch Courage	170
Face The Music	172
Fit As A Fiddle	174
Fly Off The Handle	176
Pie In The Sky	178
Touch And Go	180
Foot The Bill	182
Gone To Pot	184

Knock On Wood / Touch Wood 186
Know The Ropes 188
Top Dog and Underdog 190
Sleep Tight 192
Pipe Dream 194
Crocodile Tears 196
Hands Down 198
Tie The Knot 200
Tide You Over 202
White Elephant 204

Introduction

If you've ever found yourself pondering the strange tapestry of words and phrases that the English language has given us, you're in for a treat.

Welcome to "Why We Say The Things We Say", where the reasons behind the idioms are explained, each one being beautifully illustrated with its own unique full-color picture.

Have you ever found yourself 'on cloud nine' and wondered what happened to the other eight clouds? Or perhaps you've heard the phrase 'pull your socks up' and thought, "Why socks?"

Prepare to laugh, to wonder, and occasionally to exclaim, "Ah, now I get it!" As you delve into these pages, you'll not only discover the origins of phrases but also connect with stories that are as human and endearing as they are amusing.

So, ready your mental ship for a voyage across the seas of sayings and oceans of orations. By the end, you won't just know why we say certain things, but you'll have stories to share, making any conversation a touch more interesting.

Rule Of Thumb

- **Meaning**: A general principle or guideline that provides practical advice or a basic method, rather than a strict or precise measure.

- **Origin**: The origin of "rule of thumb" is not definitively known, but several theories exist. One of the most widely believed is that the term originated from old English law, which allegedly allowed a man to beat his wife with a stick, provided it was no wider than his thumb. However, there's no documented evidence whatsoever of such a law ever existing and is highly likely to be an urban myth or an unfunny "jocular" comment that somehow gained momentum. A more plausible origin relates to various manual trades where workers used the width or length of their thumbs as a rough measurement. For instance, farmers and gardeners might have used their thumbs to approximate planting depths, or brewers might have used the thumb to gauge the right temperature for yeast. Over time, the phrase evolved to represent a general, non-specific guideline or heuristic in various contexts.

As Mad As A Hatter

- **Meaning**: The phrase "as mad as a hatter" is used to describe someone who is behaving in a crazy, eccentric, or irrational manner.

- **Origin**: The term "as mad as a hatter" is often mistakenly thought to originate from Lewis Carroll's "Alice's Adventures in Wonderland" because of the eccentric character known as the Mad Hatter. However, the idiom's roots predate the book and are grounded in the hat-making industry of the 18th and 19th centuries. During this period, hatters used a process involving mercurous nitrate to treat the felt used in hat-making. Prolonged exposure to mercury vapors caused many hatters to suffer from mercury poisoning, which has symptoms like tremors, slurred speech, and even hallucinations, thereby leading to erratic behavior. This association between hat-makers and erratic behavior led to the phrase "mad as a hatter." While Carroll's work popularized the term further, the original context is rooted in the historical occupational hazard faced by hatters.

Upper Hand

- **Meaning**: To have the "upper hand" means to have the advantage, control, or dominant position in a situation.

- **Origin**: The term "upper hand" is believed to have originated from various games and sports, especially those involving the use of hands. One of the most likely origins is from the old arm wrestling game, where two opponents would try to force each other's hand down onto a table, and having the "upper hand" meant you were in the winning position. Another theory suggests it could be from the game of cards, where having a superior hand of cards would put a player in a dominant position. Regardless of its precise origin, the term came to be used more broadly to denote advantage or dominance in various situations.

Who do you think is going to get the "upper hand" by forcing his opponent's hand down onto the table?

On Cloud 9

- **Meaning**: To be extremely happy or euphoric; to feel elated.

- **Origin**: The exact origin of "on cloud 9" is a bit cloudy, but there are a few theories. One of the most commonly cited explanations refers to the 1896 edition of the "International Cloud Atlas" (a book that defines cloud types). In this atlas, 'Cloud Nine' is the cumulonimbus cloud, which is the tallest of all cloud types and reaches the highest altitude (up to 30,000-40,000 feet). Being "on" this cloud would metaphorically place someone on top of the world or at a high point of happiness. Another theory suggests the phrase might have originated from the American popular music scene in the 1950s. The Temptations released a song called "Cloud Nine" in 1968, which was about euphoria, though the phrase was in use before then. Yet another theory, though less supported, points to Buddhism, where there are said to be nine levels of spiritual development, with the ninth level being the ultimate state of enlightenment and happiness. While the exact origins remain debated, the phrase has become widely recognized in the English language to describe a state of bliss or happiness.

Bluetooth

- **Meaning**: A wireless technology standard used for exchanging data between fixed and mobile devices over short distances.

- **Origin**: The term "Bluetooth" isn't an acronym or a modern technological term concocted by marketers. Its origins are rooted in ancient Scandinavian history. The name comes from a 10th-century Danish king, Harald "Bluetooth" Gormsson. Harald was instrumental in uniting Denmark and parts of Norway during his reign and was known for his skills in communication and uniting people. The name was chosen because of the technology's intent to unite various communication protocols into one universal standard. The connection between the king and the technology comes from two of the founding members of the Bluetooth Special Interest Group (SIG), Jim Kardach from Intel and Sven Mattisson from Ericsson. Kardach had read a book about Vikings where he learned about King Harald and his nickname, which he supposedly earned either because of a noticeable blue/grey tooth or his penchant for blueberries. The name "Bluetooth" was initially a code name for the project, but it eventually stuck and became the official term for the wireless technology standard.

Money For Old Rope

- **Meaning**: Earning money for something that is considered easy or trivial; making a profit with minimal effort, often from something that might be considered of little value or already used.

- **Origin**: The origins of the phrase are not definitively known, but there are several theories. One common theory suggests maritime roots. Old ropes on ships, when they were no longer fit for primary use, were taken apart for their individual fibers. These fibers, known as "oakum," were used to seal gaps in wooden ships through a process called caulking. Selling these old ropes was thus seen as a way to make money from something otherwise considered worn out. Another theory posits that it originated from times when public hangings were common, with pieces of used hanging ropes being sold as souvenirs. Yet another theory connects it to horse markets in the UK, where old horses past their prime were sold for a pittance, implying an easy profit from minimal effort. Regardless of its exact origins, the phrase has come to symbolize making easy money from seemingly worthless things.

A Quick Buck

- **Meaning**: Earning money quickly and, often, with minimal effort, sometimes through dubious or dishonest means.

- **Origin**: The term "buck" has been used as slang for the U.S. dollar since at least the mid-19th century. Its origins are somewhat debated, but one theory is that it comes from the use of deer (buck) skins as a medium of exchange in certain parts of the U.S. during the 18th century. The term "quick" in this context implies speed and ease. When combined, "a quick buck" encapsulates the idea of making money rapidly without significant effort or investment. Over time, the phrase has sometimes taken on a negative connotation, implying that the money was earned without due regard for ethics or sustained work. The expression reflects the allure of fast financial gains, often at the expense of longer-term benefits or integrity.

Peeping Tom

- **Meaning**: A person who secretly watches others, especially for inappropriate or voyeuristic reasons.

- **Origin**: The term "peeping Tom" is directly linked to the legend of Lady Godiva. According to the story, Lady Godiva, an 11th-century noblewoman in England, rode naked on horseback through the streets of Coventry to protest the oppressive taxation imposed by her husband, Leofric, the Earl of Mercia. To ensure her privacy, Lady Godiva asked all the townspeople to remain indoors and not look out. However, a tailor named Tom couldn't resist the temptation and decided to sneak a peek as she passed by. As a punishment for his voyeurism, Tom was said to have been struck blind or dead. The tale was later incorporated into English folklore, and Tom's invasive act gave rise to the term "peeping Tom" to describe someone who spies on others, especially in compromising situations.

Let Your Hair Down

- **Meaning**: To relax and behave in a free or uninhibited manner; to be oneself without pretense or restraint.

- **Origin**: This phrase dates back to an era when it was customary for women, particularly in European cultures, to wear their hair up in public, often in tight and elaborate hairstyles. Such updos were a sign of formality, modesty, or status. Letting one's hair down was typically something done in private or in a more relaxed setting. It was a way for women to relax and feel more comfortable after the constraints and formality of the day. Over time, the phrase evolved to symbolize shedding inhibitions or formalities in general, not just in the literal sense of letting down one's hair.

Kick The Bucket

- **Meaning**: A colloquial expression that means to die.

- **Origin**: The origin of "kick the bucket" has several theories: One of the most commonly cited explanations comes from the old method of slaughtering pigs. A wooden beam, often referred to as a "bucket", was used to hang the pigs by their feet for slaughter. The pig might kick the wooden beam, or "kick the bucket", in its death throes.
Another theory posits that the phrase could be derived from the Old French word 'buquet', which is a balance or a beam, but the connection between this and death isn't entirely clear. Despite the uncertainty of its origins, the phrase has been used in the English language for centuries and remains a widely recognized euphemism for dying.

Get The Sack

- **Meaning**: To be dismissed or fired from a job.

- **Origin**: The phrase "get the sack" is believed to have originated from the days when craftsmen or laborers would carry their own tools around in a sack or bag and if they found employment, would give their sack to the employer for safekeeping. If an employer no longer wanted or needed their services, the worker would be handed back their sack, indicating that they were dismissed and needed to gather their tools and leave. Essentially, receiving one's sack back was synonymous with being terminated from employment. This practice was particularly prevalent in times before permanent employment contracts became standard, where manual laborers and craftsmen were hired on a day-to-day basis. Over time, the phrase has evolved to generally mean being fired or let go from any position, regardless of whether tools or a sack were involved.

The Whole 9 Yards

- **Meaning**: To give or to get the full extent of something; to go all the way.

- **Origin**: The origins of "the whole 9 yards" are somewhat murky, and there have been multiple explanations offered over the years. Some of the most common theories include:

    1. World War II fighter pilots received a 9-yard chain of ammunition. When a pilot used all of his ammunition on one target, he gave it "the whole 9 yards."
    2. Tailors using 9 yards of fabric to make a high-quality suit or a piece of clothing. Thus, giving "the whole 9 yards" meant that someone was receiving the best possible product.
    3. Concrete trucks or other types of transportation where the full capacity was 9 yards, and if you used the entire truck's content, you used "the whole 9 yards."

Despite these various theories, the true origin of the phrase remains a topic of debate among etymologists, and no single explanation has been definitively proven to be the original source of the saying. The phrase is largely American in origin and became popularized in the 20th century.

Don't Look a Gift-Horse in the Mouth

- **Meaning**: Do not be ungrateful or overly critical of something given as a gift or benefit. It's considered rude to question the value of a present.

- **Origin**: This proverb is ancient and has been expressed in various cultures, including Latin texts. The phrase's logic stems from the practice of assessing a horse's age by examining its teeth. As horses age, their teeth begin to project further forward each year and give an indication of their age. If someone were to give you a horse as a gift, it would be seen as ungracious to inspect the horse's teeth immediately, as it implies one is trying to ascertain its value or age, rather than simply appreciating the gift itself. In essence, to "look a gift-horse in the mouth" would be to scrutinize a gift, rather than accept it with gratitude. The saying has been used in its current English form since the 16th century, emphasizing the importance of accepting gifts with grace and without undue scepticism.

Pardon My French

- **Meaning**: An apology given in advance of using profanity or crude language; ironically suggesting that the following crude language is in some way comparable to the French language.

- **Origin**: The phrase "Pardon my French" has its roots in the 19th century when the English and French had a historical rivalry. During this period, many English phrases and expressions included mock French terms as a form of derision. It became a trend to apologize for using French terms by saying "pardon my French" as a tongue-in-cheek apology for swearing, implying that the swear words were the "French" that needed pardoning. Over time, the phrase evolved and became a humorous way to apologize for using any form of profanity, whether or not it had any connection to the French language. It's worth noting that while this phrase might be seen as playful or humorous in its intent, it's based on an outdated cultural stereotype and might be considered in bad taste by some.

Filthy Rich

- **Meaning**: Extremely wealthy; possessing a vast amount of money or assets, often to an excessive or ostentatious degree.

- **Origin**: The term "filthy rich" is believed to have originated in the United States in the early 20th century. The word "filthy" is used here to intensify the word "rich," much in the same way that words like "dirt" can intensify other adjectives (e.g., "dirt cheap"). The adjective "filthy" often conveys something that is extreme, excessive, or tainted. When combined with "rich," it suggests not just wealth, but an overabundance or excess of it, and sometimes even implies that the wealth might have been gained through questionable or unscrupulous means. Over time, the term became a colloquial way to describe someone with an immense amount of wealth, regardless of how they acquired it.

Go Bananas

- **Meaning**: To become very excited, agitated, or angry; to act in a wild or unrestrained manner.

- **Origin**: The exact origins of the phrase "go bananas" are a bit hazy, but it's widely believed to have emerged in the United States during the 20th century. One theory suggests that the term might be related to the supposed effects of eating bananas, which are high in dopamine—a neurotransmitter that can affect mood and behavior. However, this connection is tenuous. A more likely origin is the association between bananas and monkeys. Monkeys are often depicted in popular culture as being wild and excitable, especially when presented with bananas. The chaotic behavior of monkeys when excited could have led to the phrase "go bananas" being used to describe humans acting similarly unrestrained or overly excited. The phrase gained popularity in the latter half of the 20th century and is now widely understood to mean exhibiting heightened emotions or excitement.

Happy as Larry

- **Meaning**: Extremely happy or contented.

- **Origin**: The phrase "happy as Larry" is of Australian or New Zealand origin and dates back to the late 19th century. The exact identity of "Larry" is not definitively known, and various theories have been proposed over the years. One popular theory suggests that the phrase refers to the Australian boxer Larry Foley (1847-1917). Foley was a successful pugilist who retired undefeated and subsequently won a large sum of money in a bet. His good fortune and successful career might have made him a symbol of happiness and contentment. Another theory is that "Larry" doesn't refer to any specific individual but is simply a name chosen for its catchy alliteration. Regardless of the origins, the phrase is widely used, especially in Australia and New Zealand, to describe someone who is in an exceptionally good mood or feeling very content.

Kangaroo Court

- **Meaning**: A court that ignores recognized standards of law or justice and often carries little or no official standing in the territory within which it resides. A "kangaroo court" may have biased proceedings and offer no real justice to the accused.

- **Origin**: The term "kangaroo court" originated in the United States during the 19th century, with the earliest recorded use being in the 1850s. The exact reason for the use of "kangaroo" in this context is unclear. One theory posits that it may refer to the way these mock trials would "jump" to conclusions without proper examination of evidence or following due process, much like the jumping behavior of a kangaroo. Another theory suggests that the term could be linked to the wild and unpredictable nature of the Australian outback, drawing a parallel between the unpredictability of kangaroos and the unpredictability of these unjust courts. However, it's important to note that the term is of American origin and not Australian. Over time, "kangaroo court" has become a colloquial expression for any judicial proceeding or tribunal that disregards legal rights or is perceived to be a sham or unjust.

My Ears Are Burning

- **Meaning**: A colloquial expression used when someone believes or suspects that they are being talked about, especially when they're not present to hear the conversation. It suggests that the person has a feeling or intuition that others are discussing them.

- **Origin**: This phrase has roots in ancient beliefs and superstitions. Historically, it was thought that a person's ears would become warm or start to burn if they were being talked about behind their back. In some cultures, the sensation in a specific ear might even indicate whether the talk was positive or negative. For example, a burning left ear might mean someone was speaking ill of you, while a burning right ear might indicate someone was praising you. Though we now know that there's no scientific basis for these beliefs, the phrase "my ears are burning" has endured as a playful or humorous way to acknowledge the suspicion or awareness that one is the subject of conversation.

Nineteen to the Dozen

- **Meaning**: Talking rapidly and incessantly; speaking at a very fast rate without pause.

- **Origin**: The idiom likely originates from the idea of getting more of something than is standard or expected. A dozen, meaning twelve, is a commonly recognized unit of quantity. So, to get "nineteen to the dozen" would mean receiving more than the standard amount. In the context of talking, the phrase evokes the image of words coming out more quickly than normal. Over time, the exact number in the phrase has shifted in usage and varied in different regions, but the underlying idea of speaking rapidly remains consistent. The phrase captures the essence of someone speaking so quickly that their words are exceeding the "standard rate" of speech.

$$6 + 6 = 19$$

On the Fiddle

- **Meaning**: Engaged in fraudulent or dishonest activities, especially in relation to finances or claiming undue benefits.

- **Origin**: The phrase "on the fiddle" is British slang that dates back to the 19th century. The exact etymology is not definitively known, but the term "fiddle" has historically been used in various contexts to denote deceit or trickery. For instance, a "fiddle" could refer to a small scam or fraudulent scheme. Over time, "on the fiddle" became a colloquial way to describe someone who was involved in deceitful or fraudulent activities, especially related to embezzling money or claiming benefits dishonestly. The term might evoke imagery of skillfully playing a fiddle, drawing a parallel to the dexterity required to engage in deceptive schemes.

"Hmmm. A violin with 5 strings? This guy doesn't look like he's to be trusted".

Sick as a Parrot

- **Meaning**: Extremely disappointed or dejected.

- **Origin**: The origin of the phrase "sick as a parrot" is not definitively known, but it is a uniquely British expression that became popular in the 20th century, especially within the context of football (soccer). Players, managers, or fans would often use the phrase to describe their feelings after a disappointing game or result. The imagery of a sick parrot might evoke a picture of something looking droopy, dejected, or out of sorts, similar to a person's demeanor when they're deeply disappointed. While there's no clear link between parrots and disappointment, the vivid and unusual metaphor caught on, making the phrase memorable. Over time, it has been used more broadly to express strong disappointment in various contexts, not just sports.

Takes the Biscuit/Takes the Cake

- **Meaning**: Surpasses everything; reaches the pinnacle of absurdity or incredulity. Essentially, it's used to describe something that is seen as the most extreme example of its kind, often in a negative or surprising context.

- **Origin**: The exact origin of "takes the biscuit" is somewhat nebulous, but it's believed to have roots in the 19th century. The word "biscuit" in British English refers to what Americans might call a "cookie." In various historical contexts, biscuits or other small treats were given as prizes. The term might be linked to the idea that someone or something that "takes the biscuit" has outdone others and, therefore, gets the "prize" for being the most notable in a particular way. Over time, the phrase evolved to highlight not just positive extremes, but often the absurd, ridiculous, or negative extremes of a situation. The American equivalent of this idiom is "takes the cake."

A Vicious Circle

- **Meaning**: A complex chain of events in which a result or consequence exacerbates the original problem or situation, leading to a worsening of the issue in a repetitive cycle.

- **Origin**: The phrase "a vicious circle" has its roots in logic and philosophy, dating back to the 18th century. The term was originally "vicious cycle," with "vicious" not referring to cruelty, but rather to something being flawed or ineffective. In logical terms, a "vicious circle" referred to a type of fallacious argument where the proof of one statement relied on a second statement, whose proof, in turn, relied on the first. This creates a circular form of reasoning with no solid foundation. Over time, the phrase migrated from its logical origins and began to be applied more broadly to any situation where a problem leads to a consequence that exacerbates the original problem, creating a self-perpetuating loop of negative outcomes. The term aptly captures the frustrating nature of such situations where solutions seem elusive because the problem keeps feeding on itself.

Walls Have Ears

- **Meaning**: Be cautious of what you say because others might be eavesdropping or overhearing; there's a possibility that someone is listening in on a private conversation.

- **Origin**: The phrase "walls have ears" is a cautionary reminder that conversations might not be as private as one thinks, and it has been in use for several centuries. The concept behind this idiom is ancient, emphasizing the idea that secrecy is hard to maintain and that one should always be cautious. Variations of this sentiment can be found in numerous cultures. One suggestion is that it dates back to the times of castles with secret passages, where servants or spies could listen in on conversations without being detected. Another possible origin ties it to the Château de Brissac in France during the reign of Louis XI, where the king was known to employ spies who listened behind the walls. Over time, the saying became a generalized warning about the potential lack of privacy in any setting, reminding people to be wary of where and how they discuss sensitive matters.

All Bells and Whistles

- **Meaning**: Having many extra or fancy features, often more than what is necessary; being equipped with all the latest improvements and refinements.

- **Origin**: This idiom is believed to originate from the world of ships and trains. On ships, bells and whistles were used as signals for various onboard activities, and on steam locomotives, bells and whistles served as vital communication tools to signal departures, arrivals, and warnings. When these modes of transportation had all their bells and whistles functioning, they were considered to be in top condition with all possible amenities. Over time, the phrase was adopted more broadly to describe anything that had all possible enhancements or extras, even if they might be considered superfluous. Another interpretation is that the phrase connotes the added "flash" or attention-grabbing features of a product or service, emphasizing style or flashiness over substance or necessity.

You Can Lead a Horse to Water, But You Can't Make It Drink

- **Meaning**: You can provide someone with an opportunity or give them all the resources they need, but you can't force them to take action or accept what is offered. Essentially, it underscores the limits of influence or assistance.

- **Origin**: This proverb is one of the oldest English sayings, with its roots tracing back to the 12th century. The earliest recorded mention is in "Old English Homilies" (c. 1175): "Hwa is thet mei thet hors wettrien the him self nule drinken" (Who can give water to the horse that will not drink of its own accord?). By the 16th century, the modern version of the proverb began to appear in written records. The enduring nature of this saying likely stems from its vivid imagery and the universality of its message. The straightforward scenario of leading a horse to water but not being able to compel it to drink effectively illustrates the principle that one's influence has boundaries, and individual choice or will cannot be overridden.

In the Doghouse

- **Meaning**: To be in trouble with someone due to one's actions, often resulting in them being out of favor or in a situation of being ignored or treated harshly.

- **Origin**: The phrase "in the doghouse" is believed to have originated in the early 20th century, though its precise origins are a bit unclear. The expression likely comes from the literal idea of a dog being sent to its small, uncomfortable house as a form of punishment or isolation. The term was popularized by its use in the 1921 silent film "The Kid," directed by and starring Charlie Chaplin. In a scene, a man is depicted sleeping in the doghouse as a result of a quarrel with his wife, providing a visual representation of the idiom. This visual helped cement the phrase in popular culture, encapsulating the idea of someone being metaphorically relegated to a similar status within human relationships — isolated, uncomfortable, and in disfavor due to some wrongdoing or misstep. Over time, it has come to be used more broadly anytime someone faces social punishment or ostracism due to their actions or decisions.

I'll Eat My Hat

- **Meaning**: A way of saying that one is absolutely sure about something. It's an expression of disbelief, suggesting that if one's prediction or statement proves to be wrong, they will do something highly unlikely or absurd, such as eating their own hat.

- **Origin**: This saying has been a part of English colloquialisms for several centuries. The phrase likely stems from the inherent absurdity of the idea; hats, especially in older times, were made of materials that were clearly inedible, like leather or felt. Thus, the prospect of eating one's hat was a vivid way of emphasizing certainty, as doing so would be an extreme act. The earliest recorded usage can be traced back to the 18th century. For example, in "The Card" (1911) by Arnold Bennett, a character proclaims, "If this hat is not in Longshaw market-place at two o'clock to-morrow afternoon, I'll eat it." Over time, the phrase has persisted in the language as a colorful way to underscore confidence or certainty in a statement or prediction.

A Bun In the Oven

- **Meaning**: An informal and colloquial way of saying that someone is pregnant.

- **Origin**: This phrase, "a bun in the oven," is believed to have originated in the mid-20th century and serves as a metaphorical representation of the process of baking and pregnancy. Just as a bun bakes and grows in an oven, a baby grows and develops in a mother's womb. The warm, enclosed environment of the oven serves as an allegory for the womb. The term "oven" in relation to a woman's womb can be found in various older literary sources, but the specific phrase linking it to a "bun" became popular in the 20th century. The playful and indirect nature of the expression makes it a light-hearted alternative to more straightforward terms for pregnancy. Over time, the phrase has been embraced and used commonly, especially in casual conversations or to break the news of a pregnancy in a jovial manner.

A Fish Out of Water

- **Meaning**: Describing someone who is in a situation that they are unfamiliar with or ill-prepared for, making them feel awkward or out of place.

- **Origin**: The phrase "a fish out of water" comes from the literal observation of a fish being taken out of its natural environment: water. When a fish is removed from water, it struggles, gasps, and flops around, visibly out of its element and in distress. This image serves as a vivid metaphor for a person who feels similarly out of place or uncomfortable in a particular setting or situation. The phrase has been used in this metaphorical sense since the early 15th century. The notion of feeling out of one's depth, or in unfamiliar territory, is easily visualized by the struggles of a fish on land, making the saying both evocative and easy to understand. Over the centuries, it has become a common idiom in the English language to describe feelings of discomfort or disorientation in unfamiliar environments.

Right-Hand Man

- **Meaning**: A person's most trusted assistant or second-in-command, someone who is indispensable and extremely reliable.

- **Origin**: The term "right-hand man" draws from the cultural and historical preference for the right hand over the left. In many cultures, the right hand has traditionally been associated with trustworthiness, honor, and strength. This bias can be seen in multiple aspects, from religious texts to daily practices. The right hand is often considered the dominant hand, the hand of action, and the hand with which oaths were sworn or battles fought. Historically, a leader's shield-bearer (in battle) would stand to their left, allowing the leader to wield a weapon with their dominant right hand. Thus, the person on their right would be a trusted companion or the next in line, ready to defend or take action. By the 16th century, the term "right hand" was being used in a figurative sense to mean "the most valuable or reliable." By the 17th century, "right-hand man" was used to describe a chief assistant or indispensable colleague. Over time, this expression was adopted into common parlance to describe someone's main aide or most trusted individual.

A Bird in the Hand is Worth Two in the Bush

- **Meaning**: It's better to have a certain advantage or a more modest, assured outcome than the mere potential of a greater one. Essentially, it stresses the value of possessing something tangible now rather than hoping for something bigger and better in the future.

- **Origin**: This proverbial saying has its roots in ancient times, with the earliest known written version appearing in a compendium of proverbs by the Greek author Aesop in the 6th century B.C. The essence of the saying is present in one of his fables, "The Hawk and the Nightingale," in which a nightingale is caught by a hawk and tries to bargain for its life by offering to sing a beautiful song. The hawk replies that he would be a fool to let go of a bird he already has for the promise of a song. The exact phrasing as we know it today appears much later in English. The earliest recorded version in English is from the 15th century, found in "The Hazelwood Book" where it says, "Better one byrde in hande than ten in the wood." Over time, the saying evolved and solidified into the well-known version we use today. The sentiment behind this proverb remains a universal lesson on the value of certainty versus potential.

Knock the Spots Off

- **Meaning**: To be vastly superior to; to outclass or outperform someone or something by a significant margin.

- **Origin**: The phrase derives from a visual metaphor. When thinking of spots on an object or animal, removing them would significantly change or improve its appearance. The phrase could also be related to games involving dice (which have spots, or pips), suggesting that to "knock the spots off" would mean rendering the dice useless or defeating the purpose of the game. Over time, the saying evolved to imply outdoing or surpassing someone or something in a remarkable way. Another theory is that it might relate to the challenge of removing stains or spots from clothing, a task that, if achieved, would demonstrate superior skill or effort. Despite the uncertainty around its exact origins, the phrase is used to describe a clear and notable superiority or advantage over someone or something else.

Sheriff

- **Meaning**: The chief executive officer in a county or some other jurisdiction who is responsible for maintaining peace and enforcing laws. Typically, a sheriff is an elected official whose duties may range from overseeing local law enforcement to administering county jails.

- **Origin**: The term "sheriff" is derived from the Old English words "scīrgerefa", where "scīr" means "shire" (which is a district or administrative division, especially in England) and "gerefa" means "reeve" (an official or chief officer in a particular district). Therefore, "scīrgerefa" can be translated as "shire reeve." In medieval England, the shire reeve was the main official of the local district, responsible for maintaining law and order, collecting taxes, and representing the king's interests. As English settlers moved to other parts of the world, including America, they brought with them their systems of governance and the position of the sheriff, though the role evolved and changed based on local needs and contexts. Today, the title "sheriff" is used in various countries, but its duties and powers can differ widely depending on the region and legal jurisdiction.

Eavesdropping

- **Meaning**: Secretly listening to a private conversation without the consent of the parties involved.

- **Origin**: The term "eavesdropping" has its roots in Old English architecture and customs. The word "eaves" refers to the overhanging edges of a roof, and "drop" or "drip" relates to the water that drips from the eaves. Traditionally, houses had a space or a boundary around them to catch the rain that fell off the eaves. This area was known as the "eavesdrip" or "eavesdrop." Someone standing within this boundary could easily overhear conversations occurring inside the house without being seen. Thus, the act of standing under the eaves to listen surreptitiously to private conversations gave rise to the term "eavesdropping." Over time, the word evolved to mean any act of secretly overhearing conversations, regardless of one's physical location relative to the eaves of a house.

Butter Someone Up

- **Meaning**: To flatter or compliment someone excessively, often with an ulterior motive or to gain favor.

- **Origin**: The phrase "butter someone up" is believed to have ancient origins. In ancient India, it was a customary practice to throw balls of clarified butter at statues of gods to seek favor and blessings. By "buttering" up the statues, devotees hoped to appease the deities and ensure good fortune. In a similar vein, in the pre-Christian era among the Celts, butter was used to anoint stone idols in the hopes of receiving blessings from the gods. The modern usage, referring to flattery and charm directed towards people rather than deities, has taken on a slightly more cynical tone. It implies insincerity or the use of praise and compliments as a form of manipulation to get something one desires. The figurative sense of the phrase as we understand it today appears to have been used in English since at least the 19th century. The analogy being drawn is that just as butter makes things smooth, flattery can smooth one's way with another person.

Let The Cat Out Of The Bag

- **Meaning**: To reveal a secret or a surprise, usually unintentionally.

- **Origin**: The phrase "let the cat out of the bag" has an intriguing origin tied to old market practices. In medieval England, piglets were often sold in markets. Once a purchase was made, the piglet was placed in a bag for the buyer to take home. However, some unscrupulous sellers would replace the piglet with a less valuable cat when the buyer wasn't looking. If someone inadvertently opened the bag before reaching home, the scam would be revealed, literally "letting the cat out of the bag". Over time, the phrase evolved to have a more general meaning, referring to the disclosure of any secret, rather than just the specific market scam.

Pull Your Socks Up

- **Meaning**: An exhortation to improve one's behavior, attitude, or performance.

- **Origin**: The origin of "pull your socks up" is somewhat literal in nature and is tied to the habits and standards of personal appearance. In earlier times, particularly in the 19th century, long socks were commonly worn. If someone's socks had slipped down, it was considered sloppy or a sign of laziness. Pulling one's socks up was a quick way to improve one's appearance and show a sense of order and discipline. The act became symbolic of correcting oneself or making an effort to improve in other areas of life. Over time, the phrase evolved from this literal action to a metaphorical one, urging someone to improve or correct their ways in a broader sense, whether it be in performance, behavior, or attitude.

Spill The Beans

- **Meaning**: To reveal a secret or disclose confidential information, often unintentionally.

- **Origin**: The origin of "spill the beans" is believed to have American roots. One theory suggests the phrase originates from an ancient Greek voting method where white and black beans were used. A white bean indicated a positive vote, and a black bean was negative. If the container was knocked over, or the beans were spilled, the outcome would be prematurely revealed. Another theory points to the agricultural practice of knocking over a container of beans and, thereby, revealing its contents. Over time, this act of accidental revelation became metaphorical, symbolizing the act of unintentionally revealing a secret.

A Flash In The Pan

- **Meaning**: Something that shows potential or looks promising initially but ultimately fails to deliver or succeed; a short-lived success or phenomenon.

- **Origin**: The phrase "A flash in the pan" has its roots in the old flintlock firearms used in the 16th to 19th centuries. These guns had a small pan where gunpowder was placed. When the trigger was pulled, the flint would strike steel, creating a spark to ignite the powder. Ideally, this would then ignite the main charge of the gun and fire the bullet. However, sometimes only the powder in the pan would ignite, causing a brief flash without firing the bullet. This momentary and ineffective flash is the origin of the phrase, representing something that begins with promise but fails to deliver any meaningful or lasting result.

Dead Ringer

- **Meaning**: Someone who looks very similar to someone else; an exact duplicate or lookalike.

- **Origin**: The term "Dead Ringer" is believed to come from horse racing in the late 19th and early 20th centuries. A "ringer" was a term used for a horse that was fraudulently substituted for another in a race, essentially a horse that was an impostor. The word "dead" in this context means "exact" or "precise," as in "dead on." So a "dead ringer" would be an exact substitute or lookalike. Over time, the term expanded beyond horse racing and began to be used more broadly to describe people or things that looked nearly identical. Contrary to popular myths, the phrase has no direct association with bells, graveyards, or the deceased.

Whichever image you prefer, they both show dead ringers! 😊

Last-Ditch Attempt

- **Meaning**: A final effort or attempt, usually made when everything else has failed.

- **Origin**: The phrase "last-ditch attempt" traces its roots back to military terminology. The term "ditch" in this context refers to defensive trenches or fortifications. When soldiers made a "last-ditch" stand, they were defending their final line of defense or making a desperate stand against the enemy when all other defenses had been breached. Over time, the term began to be used metaphorically to describe any desperate, final attempt made in difficult circumstances. The word "last" emphasizes the finality and desperation of the situation.

The horrors of war.

Paint The Town Red

- **Meaning**: To go out and enjoy oneself flamboyantly, often by going to various establishments and celebrating with great enthusiasm.

- **Origin**: The expression "paint the town red" is believed to have originated from the wild behavior of the Marquis of Waterford, a British nobleman, and his companions in 1837. After a day of drinking, they supposedly went on a spree in the town of Melton Mowbray, committing various acts of vandalism, one of which was painting many of the town's buildings, including a tollgate and a swan statue, with red paint. The phrase captured the idea of unrestrained merrymaking and was popularized to mean celebrating in a lively and uninhibited manner. Over time, it became associated with revelry and boisterous fun, often in nightlife settings.

Hell For Leather

- **Meaning**: At top speed; as fast as possible.

- **Origin**: The phrase "hell for leather" is believed to originate from British military slang in the late 19th century, with references to it appearing in literature around the 1880s and 1890s. The term "leather" in the phrase refers to horse tack, specifically saddles and other riding equipment. Riding "hell for leather" implied riding a horse extremely fast and recklessly, likely to the point where both the rider and the horse's leather equipment suffered wear and tear. The association with "hell" emphasized the wild or unrestrained speed. The phrase gained wider popularity through Western novels and movies, emphasizing fast and reckless horse riding.

Caught Red-Handed

- **Meaning**: To catch someone in the act of doing something wrong or illegal, especially in a situation where they are visibly guilty.

- **Origin**: The phrase "caught red-handed" has its roots in ancient laws related to butchery and theft. During the Middle Ages in Scotland, laws existed that punished people for butchering an animal that didn't belong to them. If someone was suspected of such a crime, having blood on their hands was considered strong evidence of guilt, as it would indicate that they had recently cut up an animal. Thus, to be found with "red hands" meant that a person was caught in the act, with the evidence quite literally on their hands. Over time, the phrase evolved and expanded in its application and came to be used more generally to indicate someone caught in the act of a crime or wrongdoing, regardless of whether it involved butchery.

Out Of The Blue

- **Meaning**: Unexpectedly; without warning or preparation; suddenly.

- **Origin**: The phrase "out of the blue" is believed to be derived from the full expression "a bolt from the blue" or "a bolt out of the blue", which describes a sudden and unexpected event. The "blue" in the expression refers to the blue sky, which is calm and clear. When a bolt, often interpreted as a lightning bolt, suddenly strikes from this clear sky, it's unexpected. This metaphorically relates to unexpected surprises or shocks in life. Over time, the shortened form "out of the blue" became more popular and synonymous with something happening unexpectedly. The phrase is a testament to how nature and its unpredictable forces have influenced the way we express unexpected occurrences in our own lives.

Stinking Rich

- **Meaning**: Extremely wealthy.

- **Origin**: The phrase "stinking rich" is believed to have origins that date back to medieval times in Europe. One theory suggests that it relates to the burial practices of the wealthy. The rich could afford to be buried in crypts inside or beneath churches rather than in graveyards outside. Over time, as bodies decayed, a foul smell could permeate the church, leading locals to say the "stink" was the result of the wealthy buried below. Hence, the wealthy became associated with the term "stinking rich". Another theory is less literal and suggests that the phrase simply combines "stinking" as an intensifier with "rich" to mean "very rich". While the exact origin remains debated, the phrase has come to colloquially describe someone with immense wealth, often with a slightly negative or envious connotation.

At The Drop Of A Hat

- **Meaning**: Immediately; without any hesitation; on the slightest signal or urging.

- **Origin**: The expression "at the drop of a hat" is believed to have originated in the 19th century in the United States. The exact roots are a bit ambiguous, but one popular theory is that it is linked to the practice of dropping a hat as a signal for a race or fight to begin. Hats were used because they could be easily seen by all participants. When the hat was dropped, the event would start instantly. Over time, the phrase evolved to mean doing something without delay or hesitation. So, to do something "at the drop of a hat" means to do it immediately, without needing any further prompting or preparation.

A Feather In Your Cap

- **Meaning**: An achievement or something to be proud of; a special honor or recognition for an accomplishment.

- **Origin**: The phrase "a feather in your cap" dates back to a time when warriors would add a feather to their helmets or caps as a mark of honor or to signify an achievement, typically after defeating an opponent in battle. In various cultures, adding feathers to one's headgear has historically represented accomplishments, acts of bravery, or other significant feats. For example, in some Native American tribes, warriors earned feathers for acts of valor and would wear them proudly as symbols of their achievements. Similarly, in Europe, archers sometimes received a feather for their accomplishments. Over time, the practice transformed into a metaphorical phrase, suggesting that someone has done something noteworthy or commendable. Thus, to have "a feather in your cap" means to have achieved something of distinction or recognition.

Quantum Leap

- **Meaning**: A sudden, significant, or dramatic advance or improvement; a breakthrough.

- **Origin**: The term "quantum leap" originates from quantum mechanics, a branch of physics that studies the behavior of particles on an incredibly small scale, often at the atomic or subatomic level. In this scientific context, a "quantum" is the smallest possible discrete unit of any physical property, and a "quantum leap" refers to the sudden and discontinuous transition of an electron from one energy state to another within an atom. This change happens instantaneously without the electron appearing in the intermediate states between the two energy levels. Though the change in the electron's energy state is minuscule, it is significant in quantum mechanics. Over time, this scientific term was adopted into popular language to describe any significant or sudden advance, especially in knowledge or technique, even though in its original context, ironically, it referred to something very small. The term is often used today in a more figurative sense to indicate a major step forward or breakthrough in various fields.

A Red Letter Day

- **Meaning**: A significant or memorable day, often due to something important or special happening.

- **Origin**: The expression "a red letter day" dates back to ancient Roman times when important days were highlighted in red on calendars. This practice continued through medieval Europe. In particular, early Christian calendars marked saints' days and other significant religious events in red, a tradition that became especially prevalent with the advent of printed calendars. The term "red letter" comes from the use of red ink to highlight these significant dates. Over time, the phrase evolved to refer to any day of special significance or importance, not just religious events. Today, it is used more broadly to signify any memorable or especially important day in one's life.

On A Wing And A Prayer

- **Meaning**: Proceeding or continuing with a venture or activity with very little chance of success, often relying on hope and determination rather than concrete means or resources.

- **Origin**: The phrase "on a wing and a prayer" has its origins in World War II, particularly with the aircrews of bomber planes. After enduring combat and sustaining damage, many aircraft would attempt to return to their bases, often in very poor condition. The hope of making it back safely with limited functionality was like "limping home on a wing and a prayer." The term became popularized by the song "Comin' In On A Wing And A Prayer" in 1943, which was about such damaged aircrafts returning from missions. The song was a hit during the war and helped to solidify the phrase in popular language. Over time, it has come to describe any situation where success is uncertain and relies heavily on hope or luck.

The $64,000 Question

- **Meaning**: This phrase refers to a very important or fundamental question. It's often used to highlight a pivotal or crucial issue that needs to be addressed or answered.

- **Origin**: "The $64,000 Question" has its roots in a popular American radio quiz show from the 1940s named "Take It or Leave It." Contestants on this show could win increasing amounts of money by answering successively harder questions, with the top prize being $64. This amount might seem small now, but it was significant during that time. The show's format was later adapted for television in the 1950s and renamed "The $64,000 Question," reflecting the increased prize money. The show was extremely popular, and the phrase "The $64,000 Question" entered popular language as a way to describe a crucial or defining question. Over the years, even as the actual monetary value became less significant due to inflation, the term remained in use to denote an all-important query.

In Seventh Heaven

- **Meaning**: The expression "in seventh heaven" means to be in a state of extreme joy, happiness, or contentment.

- **Origin**: The origin of the phrase "in seventh heaven" can be traced back to ancient religious beliefs, particularly those found in Judaism, Islam, and the mystical aspects of various religions. In these traditions, there are multiple levels or heavens, with each level being more sacred and closer to God than the previous. In particular, the concept of seven heavens is a common belief in Islamic and Jewish cosmologies. The seventh heaven, being the highest and most exalted of these layers, is where God resides and is the epitome of joy and divine connection. Thus, being "in seventh heaven" symbolizes the pinnacle of happiness and ecstasy, akin to being in the most divine and perfect place possible. Over time, this religious imagery has been adopted into secular language to express an extreme state of happiness or contentment.

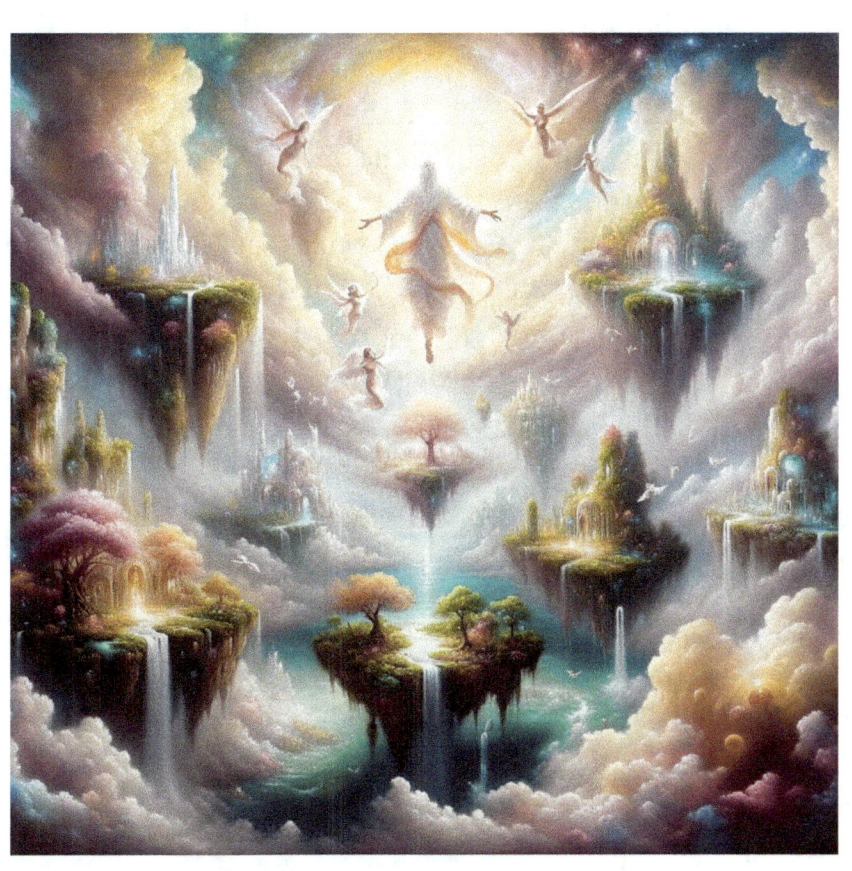

Close, But No Cigar

- **Meaning**: The phrase "close, but no cigar" is used to indicate that someone has fallen just short of a successful outcome or has come close to achieving a goal but ultimately did not succeed.

- **Origin**: The origin of the phrase "close, but no cigar" is believed to come from the carnivals and fairs of the late 19th and early 20th centuries in the United States. At these events, games of skill or chance were often played, with the winner receiving a prize. In many cases, the prizes for these games were cigars. If a participant came close to winning but didn't quite meet the mark, they might be told "close, but no cigar," highlighting the fact that they were near success but did not earn the prize. The expression was popularized further in movies and other media during the 20th century and eventually became a common idiom used to indicate a near miss or a situation where success was almost achieved but not quite.

Catch 22

- **Meaning**: The term "catch-22" describes a paradoxical situation or problem in which an individual cannot avoid because of contradictory constraints or rules. It often refers to a situation where a solution is impossible due to inherently illogical or contradictory conditions.

- **Origin**: The phrase "catch-22" originates from the 1961 novel "Catch-22" by Joseph Heller. In the novel, the term is used to describe a military regulation that presents soldiers with a circular, no-win scenario regarding mental health. Specifically, if a soldier requests a mental fitness evaluation to determine if they're insane and thus unfit for service, the very act of making the request proves they are sane (because it is considered sane to want to avoid combat). Therefore, there's no way for the soldier to escape dangerous duty. The novel, which satirized the absurdity and bureaucracy of war and military life, popularized the term, and it soon began to be applied to other paradoxical situations outside of the book's context.

Carry The Can

- **Meaning**: To "carry the can" means to take responsibility, especially for something that has gone wrong or for the actions of others.

- **Origin**: The origins of the phrase "carry the can" are believed to have nautical roots. In maritime contexts, a 'can' referred to a container or buoy, and sailors would have to carry or handle these cans during their duties. Another theory suggests that it relates to workers carrying containers or cans of milk or other produce, and thus bearing the responsibility for its safe delivery. Over time, the term evolved to represent taking responsibility or blame in a broader sense, not limited to its literal meaning. The phrase became particularly popular in the UK and has been used in various contexts to signify accountability or blame.

Okay/OK

- **Meaning**: "Okay" (often abbreviated as "OK") signifies agreement, acceptance, approval, or acknowledgment. It can be used as an adjective meaning satisfactory or acceptable, as a verb meaning to approve, or as an interjection to express agreement or acknowledgment.

- **Origin**: The origins of "okay" are diverse, and multiple theories attempt to explain its etymology. One of the most popular theories suggests that "OK" comes from the humorous misspelling of "all correct" as "oll korrect" which was a fad in Boston in the late 1830s. Another theory posits that it comes from the Choctaw word "okeh" which means "it is so". Yet another theory suggests it may have originated from a telegraphic code indicating "open key," or from the initials of a railroad freight agent, Orrin Kendall. Despite these various theories, the "oll korrect" origin is the most widely accepted and recognized, especially because the term gained popularity after being used in a campaign by U.S. President Martin Van Buren, who was nicknamed "Old Kinderhook" (OK). Regardless of its beginnings, "okay" has become one of the most universally recognized words in the world.

As Bright As A Button

- **Meaning**: The phrase "as bright as a button" describes someone who is lively, alert, intelligent, or quick-witted.

- **Origin**: The expression has two potential sources of origin. Firstly, the term "bright" in Old English could mean both "shiny" and "smart", so the phrase could originally have described the gleaming appearance of buttons, especially those that had been polished and shined. Over time, it might have evolved to relate to someone's sharpness of mind, likening a person's brightness or alertness to the shine of a well-polished button. Secondly, there's also the possibility that the "button" referred to in the phrase is not the kind you'd find on clothing but rather a bud or young shoot of a plant, which appears fresh and lively. However, the first theory related to shiny buttons is the more widely accepted explanation, given the long-standing tradition of associating a polished or bright appearance with freshness and vivacity.

Off The Cuff

- **Meaning**: The phrase "off the cuff" refers to something done spontaneously, without preparation or being rehearsed.

- **Origin**: The expression "off the cuff" is believed to have its origins in the early 20th-century practice of public speakers making notes on their shirt cuffs, using them as an improvised set of prompts during their speeches. Since these notes were typically made quickly and last-minute, they were not as polished or prepared as a traditional speech. As a result, "off the cuff" came to symbolize any remarks or actions that were impromptu or unrehearsed. Over time, the phrase evolved to be used in a broader context, indicating anything done without prior preparation or planning.

Laughing Stock

- **Meaning**: The term "laughing stock" refers to a person or thing that is the subject of mockery or ridicule.

- **Origin**: The word "stock" in medieval times meant a stationary object or fixture, and one of its uses was in the context of the "stocks," a form of public punishment where offenders had their ankles, and sometimes wrists, locked between two wooden boards in the public square. Being placed in the stocks was not just a punishment of restraint; it was primarily a punishment of public humiliation, as townspeople would ridicule and sometimes throw objects at the person in the stocks. Over time, the phrase "laughing stock" evolved to describe anyone or anything that was publicly mocked or made fun of, even outside of the context of the medieval punishment.

Once In A Blue Moon

- **Meaning**: The phrase "once in a blue moon" is used to describe a rare event or occurrence that doesn't happen very often.

- **Origin**: The term "blue moon" historically refers to the rare appearance of two full moons in a single calendar month, which typically happens once every 2.7 years. The moon does not actually appear blue in color. The use of the word "blue" in this context is old English slang meaning "rare." Over time, "blue moon" became synonymous with rarity, leading to the phrase "once in a blue moon" to denote something that happens infrequently. It's worth noting that there are other less common occasions where the moon can appear with a bluish hue, such as when atmospheric conditions contain particles from volcanic eruptions or large fires, but the phrase's origin is more closely tied to the occurrence of two full moons in one month.

Son Of A Gun

- **Meaning**: Originally, "son of a gun" was used as a euphemism to avoid stronger, more offensive language. Today, it is often used more light-heartedly to refer to a mischievous or cheeky person, but can also be used affectionately to refer to someone, typically a male.

- **Origin**: The exact origin of "son of a gun" is debated, but one popular theory dates back to the age of sail and the British navy. On ships, women were occasionally allowed on board, and if they gave birth, it would sometimes happen between the guns on the gun deck, as it was a more secluded and protected area. If the paternity of the child was in question, it might be recorded as "son of a gun." Over time, the term came to be used more broadly as a colloquialism. Another theory suggests the term was used in reference to soldiers or sailors in general. Regardless of its exact origins, the phrase evolved in meaning over the years and became a part of common vernacular.

Break A Leg

- **Meaning**: Used as a way of wishing someone good luck, especially before a performance.

- **Origin**: The exact origins of "break a leg" are somewhat murky, and multiple theories abound. One popular theory stems from the theatre world, where it's considered bad luck to wish someone "good luck." To counteract this, people would wish bad luck upon performers, hoping the opposite would occur. Next, breaking a leg refers to an actor bending his or her leg at the knee, so having to perform this action multiple times due to a well-received performance could result in injury to a leg. Yet another theory ties the phrase to the old vaudeville era. In vaudeville, performers only got paid if they actually performed on stage. "Breaking the leg" meant crossing the off-stage barrier (known as the leg) onto the stage, ensuring that they would get paid. Finally, in the theatre, a "leg" is the name of a curtain, and a highly successful run with repeated curtain calls could wear out the fly machinery that raises and lowers the "leg" or curtain. So in this case, "Break a leg" is a way of expressing your wish that the audience demands so many curtain calls, that it breaks that "leg"/curtain. While the true origin remains debated, the term is universally accepted as a wish for good fortune and success.

Spin Doctor

- **Meaning**: A person (often a media or public relations professional) who is skilled in presenting events, actions, or controversial issues in a particular, often positive or self-serving, light.

- **Origin**: The term "spin doctor" has its roots in the world of politics and media. "Spin" in this context refers to the act of presenting or interpreting an event in a particular way, often to influence public opinion. The "doctor" part of the term implies that the individual is skilled at "curing" or altering the perception of potentially damaging news or events. The term began gaining traction in the 1980s, especially in the U.S., where it was used to describe advisors to politicians who were skilled in manipulating media coverage to their advantage. Their job was to "spin" negative news into something more favorable for their client or cause. The combination of "spin" (as in twisting or turning a narrative) and "doctor" (someone who fixes or mends things) effectively captures the essence of what these individuals do – they "treat" or "fix" potentially damaging stories to make them appear more favorable.

Spitting Image

- **Meaning**: Someone who looks extremely similar to another person, often used to describe a child's strong resemblance to a parent.

- **Origin**: The phrase "spitting image" has a somewhat debated origin, but it's believed to have evolved over time from various expressions that convey close resemblance. One theory is that it derived from "spit and image," where "spit" would mean a perfect likeness, suggesting that someone is so similar they are as if made from the spit of another. Another possible origin is the phrase "spitten image," which might have come from "spirit and image," indicating that someone was alike in both spirit and appearance. Over time, these phrases morphed into the more commonly used "spitting image." Regardless of its exact roots, the term has been widely used since the 19th century to denote a striking resemblance between two individuals.

The Living Daylights

- **Meaning**: One's senses, wits, or vitality. The phrase is often used in the context of frightening or beating someone, as in "scare the living daylights out of someone" or "beat the living daylights out of someone."

- **Origin**: The term "daylights" originally referred to the eyes in the 18th century. In this context, "daylights" symbolized the windows to one's consciousness or life. The addition of "living" to the phrase emphasized the intensity or severity of a situation, making "the living daylights" a more vivid and dramatic expression. By the 19th century, the term was popularized, especially in the context of fear or threats, indicating an intense scare or beating that could threaten the very life or senses of someone. Over time, it has retained this emphasis on extremity or intensity in various contexts.

A Barrel Of Laughs

- **Meaning**: Something or someone that is very funny or entertaining.

- **Origin**: The exact origin of the phrase "a barrel of laughs" is not entirely clear, but it belongs to a family of idioms that use "barrel" to denote an abundance or large quantity of something. Barrels, historically, have been used to store and transport goods, including food and drink, so they are associated with plentifulness. The use of "barrel" in this idiomatic sense plays on the notion of an overflowing or abundant amount of laughter. The phrase became popular in the 20th century and is used to suggest that something is uproarious or very humorous.

Beat A Hasty Retreat

- **Meaning**: To quickly leave or withdraw from a situation, especially to avoid trouble or danger.

- **Origin**: The phrase "beat a hasty retreat" combines two concepts: "beat" and "hasty retreat". Historically, in military contexts, "beat" referred to the urgent drumming that signaled troops to move quickly or retreat. The word "hasty" emphasizes the rapidity of the action. As such, "beat a hasty retreat" originally had a military connotation, implying a quick withdrawal from the battlefield, often due to an imminent threat. Over time, the phrase transitioned from its military origins to colloquial usage, where it came to describe any quick exit or departure from an uncomfortable or challenging situation.

Zig Zag

- **Meaning**: A pattern or path that moves sharply back and forth in alternate directions; to move in such a manner.

- **Origin**: The term "zig zag" is believed to be of French origin, derived from the word "ziczac", which imitates the sound of something moving quickly back and forth. Its repetitive, onomatopoeic nature effectively describes the sharp changes in direction characteristic of a zigzag pattern. Over time, the term migrated into English usage, and its spelling was adapted to "zig zag". The term has been used in English since the late 17th century to describe patterns, paths, or motions that sharply alternate in direction.

In The Doldrums

- **Meaning**: To be in a state of stagnation, inactivity, or depression; to be in a sluggish, listless, or unproductive condition.

- **Origin**: The term "doldrums" originally referred to specific regions of the ocean near the equator where sailing ships would often become becalmed due to low winds, making navigation difficult. The word "doldrums" is believed to have been derived from the Old English "dol", meaning "foolish" or "dull", suggesting inactivity or stagnation. Sailors dreaded these regions due to the lack of consistent wind, which could leave them stranded for weeks. Over time, the term "in the doldrums" evolved to metaphorically represent periods of stagnation, inactivity, or depression in various contexts beyond just sailing.

Pay Through The Nose

- **Meaning**: To pay an excessive amount for something; to pay a high price.

- **Origin**: The origin of the phrase "pay through the nose" is somewhat unclear, with multiple theories offered. One theory suggests that it dates back to the 9th century when the Vikings conquered the Irish and imposed a nose tax on the Irish who did not pay. Those who couldn't or wouldn't pay had their noses slit. Another suggestion is that it originates from the idea that the nose represents the center or most conspicuous part of the face, implying a high price or prominent expense. However, concrete evidence for these theories is lacking. The phrase began appearing in English language literature in the 17th century, with its current figurative meaning of paying a high or exorbitant price. Regardless of its exact roots, the phrase conveys the sense of paying dearly or excessively for something.

Long-Winded

- **Meaning**: Being tediously prolonged or extended; verbose; using an excessive number of words to express a point or idea.

- **Origin**: The term "long-winded" has its origins in the literal sense of "having a long breath or respiratory power". In the past, "wind" was a term that referred to breath or breathing, especially during physical exertion. Over time, the phrase transitioned from referring to physical breath to describing speech or writing that is drawn out, much like how someone with a lot of "wind" or breath might keep talking without pause. The term began to be used in a figurative sense to describe someone who speaks or writes in a lengthy and tedious manner. The adaptation from a physical characteristic to a characteristic of speech or writing emphasizes the tiresome nature of overly extended discourse.

The Real McCoy

- **Meaning**: The genuine article; something authentic or of high quality.

- **Origin**: The origin of "the real McCoy" is debated, but there are a couple of dominant theories. One of the most widely circulated explanations involves Elijah McCoy, a 19th-century Canadian-American inventor. He created an automatic lubricator for steam engines that was of such superior quality that railroad engineers and machinists would request "the real McCoy" to distinguish it from inferior imitations. Another theory posits that the phrase comes from the world of boxing. In the early 20th century, a welterweight champion named Kid McCoy was rumored to have been challenged in a bar by someone doubting his identity, leading to a swift knockout by the boxer and the declaration that he was "the real McCoy." However, the phrase's true origin remains uncertain, with these and other theories continuing to be explored. What's clear is that by the early 20th century, "the real McCoy" was widely understood to mean the genuine article or something of high quality.

Dressed Up To The Nines

- **Meaning**: Dressed very elegantly or flamboyantly; wearing one's finest clothes.

- **Origin**: The phrase "dressed up to the nines" has an uncertain origin, though there are several theories. One of the more commonly accepted explanations relates to the length of fabric used to make a suit or outfit. A tailor would use nine yards of material to create a suit, which would be of the finest quality. To be "dressed to the nines" thus meant that someone was wearing a very fine suit made from a lot of fabric. Another theory ties the phrase to the number nine's historical association with perfection or completeness, as in "the whole nine yards." In this case, "to the nines" would simply mean "to perfection" or "to the utmost degree." Another suggestion is that it comes from the 99th Wiltshire Regiment, known for its smart appearance. Despite the various theories, the precise origin remains unclear. The phrase has been in use since the late 18th century and has always denoted excellence or high standards in appearance.

Gift Of The Gab

- **Meaning**: The ability to speak easily and confidently in a way that makes people want to listen to you and believe you; a talent for verbal fluency.

- **Origin**: The phrase "gift of the gab" has its roots in Irish folklore. According to legend, anyone who kissed the Blarney Stone, a block of limestone built into the battlements of Blarney Castle near Cork, Ireland, would be endowed with the gift of eloquence or persuasive speech. The word "gab" is an old slang term for speech or conversation, which can be traced back to Middle English. Over time, "gift of the gab" came to describe someone who had a way with words, whether they had visited the Blarney Stone or not. The phrase encapsulates the idea that the ability to speak persuasively and charmingly is a special talent or "gift".

Hedge Your Bets

- **Meaning**: To protect oneself against loss by supporting more than one side or outcome, especially in a bet or wager; to avoid committing fully to one option in order to leave open other possibilities.

- **Origin**: The phrase "hedge your bets" is derived from the term "hedge" in relation to finance and investment, where it means to limit or qualify (something) by conditions or exceptions. Originally, a "hedge" was a fence made up of interwoven branches or bushes, designed to enclose a piece of land. Over time, the term began to be used figuratively in the sense of a boundary or limit. In the 16th century, "hedging" was used in the context of buying and selling commodities to mean the avoidance of a strict commitment to an investment. For instance, a merchant who expected to receive a shipment of a certain commodity might "hedge" by also making a corresponding sale of the same commodity, offsetting the risk of price changes. By the 17th century, this concept was applied to betting: to "hedge one's bets" was to place bets on opposing outcomes, thus reducing the risk of a large loss. The phrase has since become a popular idiom in everyday language, signifying the action of reducing one's risks or protecting oneself from total failure.

Give Up The Ghost

- **Meaning**: To die or cease to function; to stop working or operating; to give out or fail.

- **Origin**: The phrase "give up the ghost" originates from the Bible, where it was used to describe a person's final moment of life or the act of dying. In several translations of the Bible, the term "ghost" was used as a synonym for "spirit" or "soul". For instance, in the King James Version of the Bible, when Jesus dies on the cross, it's said that "Jesus, when he had cried again with a loud voice, yielded up the ghost" (Matthew 27:50). This means Jesus released his spirit, indicating his passing away. Similarly, other biblical figures are described as "giving up the ghost" upon their death. Over time, the phrase became a euphemism for dying or death. Moreover, the expression was later expanded to describe the end of non-living things, such as machines or devices, when they stop functioning. The usage of "ghost" to mean "life" or "soul" can be traced back to Old English, emphasizing the deep-rooted nature of this idiom in the English language.

Wooden Spoon

- **Meaning**: A mock or symbolic award given to the individual or team finishing last in a competition. Alternatively, it refers to a real wooden spoon, often used in cooking.

- **Origin**: The term "wooden spoon" has its roots in the academic traditions of Cambridge University, dating back to the early 19th century. At that time, it was a custom to award a wooden spoon to the student who achieved the lowest passing mark in the final year of the mathematics honors degree, known as the Mathematical Tripos. This spoon was presented in a humorous manner during graduation. Over time, the wooden spoon became synonymous with coming last in other contexts outside of Cambridge University. In sporting events, particularly in rugby, the team that finishes at the bottom of the league or tournament is often colloquially said to have "won" the wooden spoon. The original practice at Cambridge ended in the 1900s, but the term has endured and is now widely used to denote last place in various competitive contexts. While the use of the term in a competitive sense is largely British, the phrase has been adopted in other cultures and settings, often with a sense of humor attached to it.

Red Herring

- **Meaning**: A misleading clue or distraction that diverts attention away from the actual issue, typically used in the context of a narrative or argument.

- **Origin**: The term "red herring" traces back to an old technique of training hunting dogs. A smoked and dried herring fish, which turns a reddish-brown color, was dragged across the trail to divert the dogs from the scent of the game they were hunting. This was done to test and improve the dog's ability to follow a scent without being distracted. Over time, this practice was metaphorically applied to describe any kind of diversion or distraction from the main issue or topic. By the 19th century, the term was solidified in its figurative sense, with writers and journalists using "red herring" to denote a misleading or irrelevant factor introduced into a discussion or narrative to divert attention from the central issue. The metaphorical application of the term has since overshadowed its original literal meaning, and today it is widely used to denote any form of distraction or misleading element, especially in literature, films, and debates.

A well-read herring!

Pound Of Flesh

- **Meaning**: A debt ruthlessly demanded, often at great cost or harm to the debtor, and exacted in a determined, relentless manner. It usually implies a form of retribution that is excessive or without mercy.

- **Origin**: The term "pound of flesh" originates from William Shakespeare's play "The Merchant of Venice," written in the late 16th century. In the play, the character Shylock, a Jewish moneylender, agrees to lend money to Antonio under the condition that if Antonio cannot repay the loan, Shylock will be entitled to a pound of Antonio's flesh. The agreement is made as a kind of vengeful jest since Shylock harbors resentment against Antonio for multiple reasons, including Antonio's anti-Semitic views. As the story progresses, Antonio's ships are believed to be lost at sea, leading him to default on the loan. Shylock, with legal backing, then demands his pound of flesh. However, he's eventually outwitted in court when it's pointed out that the agreement allowed him to take flesh, but no blood. Since it's impossible to extract a pound of flesh without shedding blood, Shylock's claim is nullified. The phrase has since entered the English language to describe a harsh, unyielding demand for a payment or retribution.

Bite The Bullet

- **Meaning**: To bravely face a difficult or unpleasant situation, or to accept something difficult or unpleasant without complaining.

- **Origin**: The expression "bite the bullet" is believed to have originated during the times of war when soldiers, undergoing surgery in the field without anesthesia, would bite on a bullet to endure the pain and to prevent themselves from crying out. The bullet, being solid and bite-resistant, acted as a distraction and a way to cope with the intense pain. By biting on a bullet, a soldier could stifle his screams, avoid disturbing other soldiers, and show his toughness. Over time, the phrase began to be used metaphorically to refer to someone dealing with a difficult or unpleasant situation head-on, without trying to avoid it or complain about it.

Draw A Blank

- **Meaning**: To fail to recall a memory or to fail to achieve a desired outcome; to get no response or result.

- **Origin**: The phrase "draw a blank" originates from the British lottery, known as "blanks and prizes", which was popular in the 16th century. In this lottery, participants would draw slips of paper from a container, hoping to pull a slip that had a prize designation. However, many of the slips were blank, meaning the person did not win anything. Thus, if someone drew a slip without a prize, they "drew a blank". Over time, the expression began to be used more broadly to indicate a lack of success or result in various contexts, including trying to remember something and coming up empty-handed.

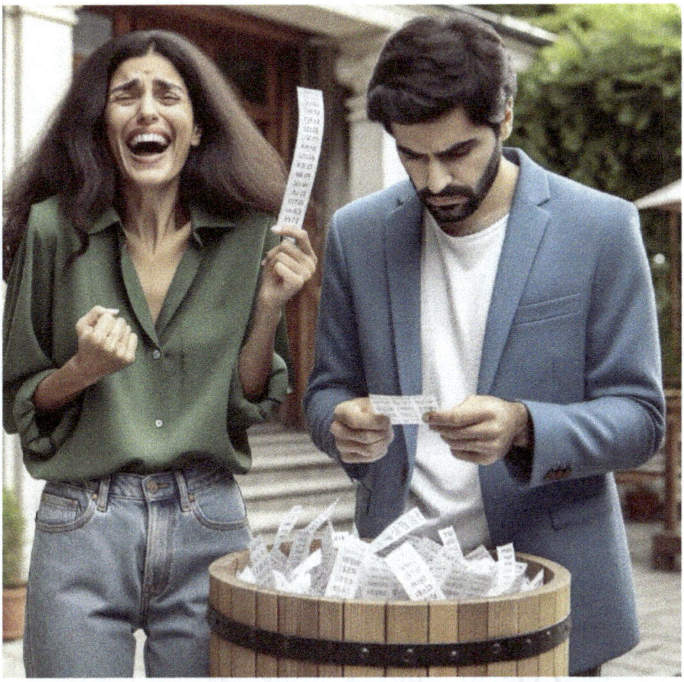

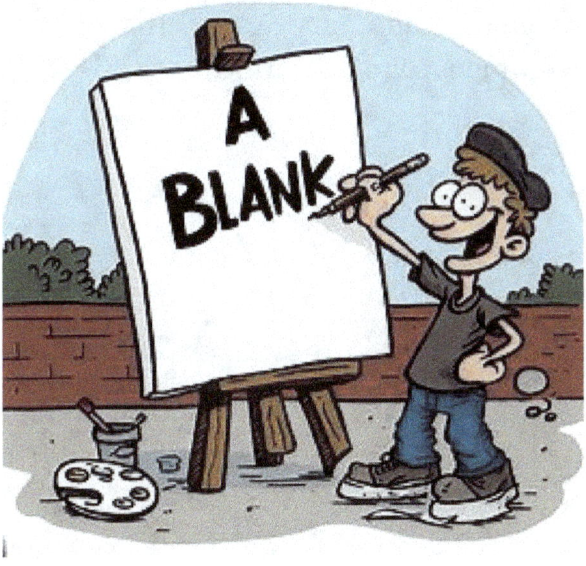

Sorry, I couldn’t resist! 😊

Dutch Courage

- **Meaning**: A false sense of bravery or confidence induced by alcohol.

- **Origin**: The term "Dutch courage" has its roots in the 17th century, during the Anglo-Dutch Wars, when England and the Dutch Republic were often rivals. The English, in a somewhat derogatory manner, ascribed a number of phrases to the Dutch to mock or belittle them. The implication with "Dutch courage" was that the Dutch sailors or soldiers needed to drink alcohol in order to muster the courage to fight, suggesting that their bravery was artificial and not genuine. Over time, the phrase became more generalized and is now used to describe the temporary bravery that can come from consuming alcohol, regardless of nationality.

Face The Music

- **Meaning**: To confront or accept the unpleasant consequences of one's actions.

- **Origin**: The exact origins of the phrase "face the music" are a bit unclear, but there are several theories. One popular suggestion is that it comes from the world of theater. An actor who has given a poor performance would have to face the music, that is, come out for a bow in front of the orchestra and the audience, and deal with any potential boos or criticism from the crowd and looks of derision from the musicians who would be sat in the orchestra pit directly in front of the stage. Another theory posits that the phrase might have military origins, referring to a disgraced officer being dismissed or "drummed out" of his regiment to the beat of a drum. Despite the uncertainty of its exact beginnings, the phrase has come to mean facing up to difficult or uncomfortable situations, usually of one's own making.

Fit As A Fiddle

- **Meaning**: To be in very good health and physical condition.

- **Origin**: The phrase "fit as a fiddle" has been used since the 16th century, though its meaning has evolved over time. Initially, "fit" meant suitable or appropriate, as in "fit for purpose", not necessarily denoting good health. A "fiddle" is another word for a violin, and the violin, being a key instrument in many musical compositions of the day, needed to be in good condition to produce the desired sound. Over time, the meaning of "fit" shifted to indicate good health, leading to the modern interpretation of the phrase as someone being in excellent physical shape. The idea is that just as a well-cared-for violin can produce beautiful music, a person in good health can function at their best.

Fly Off The Handle

- **Meaning**: To suddenly become extremely angry or lose one's temper.

- **Origin**: The expression "fly off the handle" has its roots in the 19th-century American frontier. It alludes to the uncontrolled way a loose ax head might fly off from its handle if not securely fastened. When swinging an ax, if the head wasn't firmly attached, it could become a dangerous, unpredictable projectile. Similarly, a person who "flies off the handle" behaves in a sudden and uncontrolled manner out of anger or frustration. The phrase has been in use since at least the early 1800s to describe unpredictable anger or rag

Pie In The Sky

- **Meaning**: A promise of heaven or future success, especially one that is unlikely to be fulfilled.

- **Origin**: The phrase "pie in the sky" comes from a song written in 1911 by Joe Hill, a Swedish-American labor activist, songwriter, and member of the Industrial Workers of the World. The song, titled "The Preacher and the Slave," criticized the Salvation Army preachers who promised heaven to their followers while ignoring their immediate needs and struggles. One of the song's lines goes, "You will eat, bye and bye, In that glorious land above the sky; Work and pray, live on hay, You'll get pie in the sky when you die." The phrase then became a general term for any promise that seems too good to be true or is unlikely to come to fruition.

Touch And Go

- **Meaning**: A situation that is precarious or uncertain and could result in either success or failure.

- **Origin**: The phrase "touch and go" originally referred to ships lightly touching the seabed or other obstacles without sustaining damage. In a nautical context, when a ship would "touch" an obstruction and then "go" or move away, it was a close call, indicating a dangerous situation that was narrowly avoided. Over time, this expression was adopted more broadly to describe any situation where there was a narrow escape or a close encounter with danger, and it eventually took on its figurative sense of something that is uncertain or precarious.

Foot The Bill

- **Meaning**: To pay for something, especially when the cost is considered high or unfair.

- **Origin**: The term "foot" has been used in financial contexts since the 15th century, referring to the bottom or "foot" of a bill or tally. To "foot up" meant to add up or total columns of figures. By the 18th century, "foot the bill" came to mean not just adding up the total, but taking responsibility for paying the sum. Over time, the phrase became a colloquial way of saying that someone is covering or taking on the cost of something, often generously or begrudgingly.

Gone To Pot

- **Meaning**: Something that has deteriorated or become ruined or spoiled.

- **Origin**: The phrase "gone to pot" dates back to at least the 16th century and originally referred to the process of cutting up meat to be cooked in a pot. Over time, this idea of being "cut up" or "broken down" to be put in a pot extended metaphorically to anything that has broken down, deteriorated, or gone awry. As pots were commonly used for cooking, items or ingredients that were past their prime or no longer of standalone quality would be put into the pot for stews or soups. Hence, something that has "gone to pot" became synonymous with something that has declined in quality or condition.

Knock On Wood / Touch Wood

- **Meaning**: A gesture or expression used to ward off bad luck after making a hopeful or boastful statement, or to express a hope that a good thing will continue.

- **Origin**: This superstition has its roots in ancient pagan cultures, particularly the belief that spirits or deities resided in trees. By knocking on or touching wood, individuals sought to call upon these protective spirits or to prevent them from hearing a boastful or optimistic statement, thus preventing any ill-will or bad luck. Over time, the act became more associated with simply warding off bad luck or evil spirits, rather than directly invoking tree spirits. The phrase and its associated action have been adopted and adapted by various cultures throughout history, but the basic intent remains consistent: to avoid tempting fate and to hope for continued good fortune.

Know The Ropes

- **Meaning**: To be fully acquainted or familiar with a particular job, task, or subject; to understand the details or intricacies.

- **Origin**: This expression has maritime origins, dating back to the days of sailing ships. A ship had many ropes, and each one had a specific function. Knowing what each rope did, and how to use it, was crucial for the safe and efficient operation of the ship. When a sailor said he "knew the ropes," it meant he was experienced and understood the various tasks on the ship. Over time, this phrase was adopted into general usage to mean having a thorough understanding or expertise in a particular area or activity.

Top Dog and Underdog

- **Meaning**: "Top dog" refers to someone who is dominant, superior, or in a leading position in a particular situation or hierarchy. "Underdog", on the other hand, refers to the one at a disadvantage or expected to lose; the weaker party in a situation.

- **Origin**: The terms "top dog" and "underdog" have their origins in the world of dog fighting, which was sadly a popular entertainment in many cultures for centuries. In these fights, the dog that maintained a position on top during the struggle was typically the winning or dominant dog, hence the term "top dog". Conversely, the dog on the bottom, or the one being pinned, was the one losing or at a disadvantage, leading to the term "underdog". Over time, these phrases were adopted into general language to describe positions of dominance or subordination in various contexts, far removed from their brutal origins.

Sleep Tight

- **Meaning**: "Sleep tight" is a phrase often used to wish someone a good and restful sleep.

- **Origin**: The expression "sleep tight" has its origins in the 16th and 17th centuries. During this period, beds were often made with a wooden frame, and the mattress was supported by ropes that needed to be pulled tightly to provide a stable and even sleeping surface. If the ropes became loose, the mattress would sag, making it uncomfortable to sleep. Therefore, people would be told to "sleep tight" as a reminder or wish to have the ropes kept tight, ensuring a good night's sleep. Over time, while the construction of beds changed, the saying persisted and evolved into a general well-wishing for a restful night.

Pipe Dream

- **Meaning**: An unrealistic or fanciful hope or plan that is unlikely to come to fruition.

- **Origin**: The term "pipe dream" has its origins in the late 19th century, primarily in the United States. It alludes to the vivid and often fantastical dreams experienced by those who smoked opium. Like lead and asbestos, before it was known just how bad it was for your long-term health, opium was consumed in "opium dens" and was a popular recreational drug in both the U.S. and Europe, especially during the 19th century. It is now known to cause physical, emotional, and mental health issues, but back then they didn't realize the implications of its use. The drug was typically smoked in long pipes, and it was known to induce hallucinogenic visions or dreams in its users. These dreams were often so detached from reality that the term "pipe dream" eventually came to symbolize any improbable or unattainable fantasy.

Crocodile Tears

- **Meaning**: Insincere or fake tears or displays of sorrow.

- **Origin**: The phrase "crocodile tears" can be traced back to ancient tales and observations that crocodiles would cry while devouring their prey. This apparent juxtaposition of a fierce predator showing sorrow while eating made its way into various accounts and descriptions. One of the earliest mentions of this concept is found in the works of the ancient Greek historian Herodotus. However, it's worth noting that in reality, while crocodiles do have tear glands and can produce tears, there's no scientific evidence to suggest that they cry out of emotion or sorrow. Over time, the phrase evolved in the English language to represent a display of insincere sorrow or feigned emotion.

Hands Down

- **Meaning**: Easily and decisively; without question.

- **Origin**: The phrase "hands down" has its roots in horse racing. When a jockey is far ahead of the competition and is certain to win the race, they can relax their grip on the reins and lower their hands, thereby allowing the horse to run without any restraint. This relaxed posture indicates that the victory is so assured that the jockey doesn't even need to exert control over the horse to maintain the lead. The term then transitioned into general use, denoting an easy, uncontested victory or superiority in any context.

Tie The Knot

- **Meaning**: To get married.

- **Origin**: The phrase "tie the knot" traces its origins to various cultural and historical practices where tying a knot symbolized unity and commitment. In some cultures, the hands of the bride and groom are tied together during the wedding ceremony, symbolizing their union in matrimony. This ritual is known as "handfasting." In other cultures, physical knots in clothing or ropes were used in ceremonies to represent the binding together of two lives. Over time, "tie the knot" became a popular metaphorical expression in English to describe the act of getting married.

Tide You Over

- **Meaning**: To support or sustain someone through a short period of difficulty or shortage, until further supplies or resources are available.

- **Origin**: The term "tide" in this context doesn't refer to the ocean's tides but rather derives from an old English usage of the word meaning "a period of time" or "a season". The phrase essentially means to "pass the time" or "survive during a particular time". The maritime origin is more metaphorical; just as a ship might need to wait for the next tide to proceed, someone might need a little assistance to make it through a short period of difficulty. Over time, the phrase "tide you over" came to mean providing someone with the necessary resources or support to get through a temporary challenge or period of need.

White Elephant

- **Meaning**: An item that is costly and difficult to maintain and has little practical use or value, often an unwanted possession.

- **Origin**: The term "white elephant" originates from ancient Southeast Asian cultures where the white elephant was considered sacred and highly revered. In Siam, now modern-day Thailand, it was believed that a white elephant was an auspicious sign from the heavens. When a white elephant was discovered, it was customarily presented to the king. While it was a great honor to own a white elephant, it was also a burden. The owner couldn't use the elephant for labor or other practical tasks, but still had to provide costly care and feeding for it. Additionally, it was prohibited to sell or give away the sacred animal. As a result, the possession could potentially ruin the owner financially. Over time, the term "white elephant" came to symbolize any possession that imposes financial strain without bringing any practical benefit, and later expanded to describe something generally unwanted.

   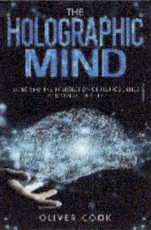 
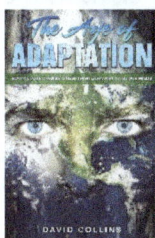    

Take a look at more great books available from Rockwood Publishing

… some for FREE!

Just visit the link below:

rockwoodpublishing.co.uk

Published by Rockwood Publishing 2023

Copyright and Trademarks. This publication is Copyright 2023 by Rockwood Publishing. All products, publications, software and services mentioned and recommended in this publication are protected by trademarks. In such instances, all trademarks & copyright belong to the respective owners. All rights reserved. No part of this book may be reproduced or transferred in any form or by any means, graphic, electronic, or mechanical, including photocopying, recording, taping, or by any information storage retrieval system, without the written permission of the author. Pictures used in this book are either royalty free pictures bought from stock-photo websites or have the source mentioned underneath the picture.

Disclaimer and Legal Notice. This product is not legal or medical advice and should not be interpreted in that manner. You need to do your own due diligence to determine if the content of this product is right for you. The author and the affiliates of this product are not liable for any damages or losses associated with the content in this product. While every attempt has been made to verify the information shared in this publication, neither the author nor the affiliates assume any responsibility for errors, omissions or contrary interpretation of the subject matter herein. Any perceived slights to any specific person(s) or organisation(s) are purely unintentional. We have no control over the nature, content and availability of the websites listed in this book. The inclusion of any website links does not necessarily imply a recommendation or endorse the views expressed within them. Rockwood Publishing takes no responsibility for, and will not be liable for, the websites being temporarily unavailable or being removed from the Internet. The accuracy and completeness of information provided herein and opinions stated herein are not guaranteed or warranted to produce any particular results, and the advice and strategies contained herein may not be suitable for every individual. The author shall not be liable for any loss incurred as a consequence of the use and application, directly or indirectly, of any information presented in this work. This publication is designed to provide information in regards to the subject matter covered. The information included in this book has been compiled to give an overview of the subject(s) and detail some of the symptoms, treatments etc. that are available to people with this condition. It is not intended to give medical advice. For a firm diagnosis of your condition, and for a treatment plan suitable for you, you should consult your doctor or consultant. The writer of this book and the publisher are not responsible for any damages or negative consequences following any of the treatments or methods highlighted in this book. Website links are for informational purposes and should not be seen as a personal endorsement; the same applies to the products detailed in this book. The reader should also be aware that although the web links included were correct at the time of writing, they may become out of date in the future.

Disclaimers

The content contained within this book is for information and entertainment purposes only, and in no way purports to represent professional medical opinion. It should NOT be used as a substitute for expert advice, and you must consult with your designated health professional before acting upon any information contained herein or before undertaking any practice whose methodology is referred to in this book. The author is NOT a registered health professional and the text merely represents personal opinion, not medical fact. The author cannot be held responsible for the consequences of any action derived from the reading of this book, as the content is not based on diagnosis and subsequent regimen. It is the reader's responsibility to seek proper, professional medical advice from a registered health practitioner in connection with any material contained within this book.

Legal Disclaimer (part 1)

Nothing in this book should be construed as an attempt to diagnose, treat or cure. The information in this book is intended to be a community resource. The author takes no responsibility for any informational material or brochures produced using information taken from this book. The author has endeavoured to ensure that all information is correct at the time of publication. This information, however, is subject to change without notice. The author makes no warranty with regard to the accuracy of any information and will not be liable for any errors or omissions. Any liability that arises as a result of this information is hereby excluded to the fullest extent allowed by law.

This information should not be used as a substitute for seeking independent professional advice.

Legal Disclaimer (part 2)

Disclaimer and Terms of Use:

a) i. In publishing this information, the author makes no representations concerning the efficacy, appropriateness or suitability of any products or treatments. Use this information at your own risk. The compiler is not a doctor and has no medical background or training.

ii. Statements and information regarding dietary supplements, books and any products mentioned have not been evaluated by any health authority and are not intended to diagnose, treat, cure or prevent any disease or health condition.

b) In view of the possibility of human error, neither the author nor any other party involved in providing this information, warrant that the information contained therein is in every respect accurate or complete and they are not responsible nor liable for any errors or omissions that may be found or for the results obtained from the use of such information. The entire risk as to use of this information is assumed by the user.

c) You are encouraged to consult other sources and confirm the information.

d) The information you access is provided "as is". No warranty, expressed or implied, is given as to the accuracy, completeness or timeliness of any information herein, or for obtaining legal advice. To the fullest extent permissible pursuant to applicable law, neither the author nor any other parties who have been involved in the creation, preparation, printing, or delivering of this information assume responsibility for the completeness, accuracy, timeliness, errors or omissions of said information and assume no liability for any direct, incidental, consequential, indirect, or punitive damages as well as any circumstance for any complication, injuries, side effects or other medical accidents to person or property arising from or in connection with the use or reliance upon any information contained herein.

e) The author is not responsible for the contents of any linked site or any link contained in a linked site, or any changes or update to such sites. The inclusion of any link does not imply endorsement by the author. The author makes no representations or claims as to the quality, content and accuracy of the information, services, products, messages which may be provided by such resources, and specifically disclaims any warranties, including but not limited to implied or express warranties of merchantability or fitness for any particular usage, application or purpose.

f) The information provided is general in nature and is intended for educational and informational purposes only. It is not intended to replace or substitute the evaluation, judgment, diagnosis, and medical or preventative care of a physician, paediatrician, therapist and/or health care provider.

g) Any medical, nutritional, dietetic, therapeutic or other decisions, dosages, treatments or drug regimes should be made in consultation with a health care practitioner. Do not discontinue treatment or medication without first consulting your physician, clinician or therapist.

h) By reading this information, you signify your assent to these terms and conditions of use. If you do not agree to these terms and conditions of use, do not read/use this information. If any provision of these terms and conditions of use shall be determined to be unlawful, void or for any reason unenforceable, then that provision shall be deemed severable from this agreement and shall not affect the validity and enforceability of any remaining provisions.

i) The information, services, products, messages and other materials, individually and collectively, are provided with the understanding that the author is not engaged in rendering medical advice or recommendations.

j) The information and the terms of use are subject to change without notice. The material provided as is without warranty of any kind and may include inaccuracies and/or typographical errors. The author makes no representations about the suitability of this information for any purpose. The author disclaims all warranties with regard to this information, including all implied warranties, and in no event shall the author be held liable, resulting from, or in any way related to, the use of this information.

k) The unauthorized alteration of the content of this information is expressly prohibited. The author, its agents and representatives shall not be responsible for any claims, actions or damages which may arise on account of the unauthorized alteration of this information.

www.ingramcontent.com/pod-product-compliance
Lightning Source LLC
Chambersburg PA
CBHW070733020526
44118CB00035B/1258